Mice Are Nice

By Sally Cowan

AF585333

Mice are small and cute.

Most mice have long faces with pink noses.

Mice have long tails.
A mouse's tail can be as long as its body.

There are lots of different types of mice!

Mice can be white, black or brown, and some have spots.

Mice build their nests in safe places.

Then the female mice have some baby mice.

A baby mouse is called a pup.

Mice can jump a long way for their size.

Mice can even swim from one place to the next.

Mice like to race about at dusk.
They can run quite fast!

The mice find plants and insects to eat.

When it is cold,
mice hunt in the frost and ice.

Mice can even dig tunnels
under snow!
They travel from place to place
that way.

We can have mice as pets.

Mice like to live where there is space to play and to hide.

This mouse has the chance to race about and have fun in this place!

Mice like to eat lots of snacks!

This mouse on the right has a slice of pumpkin.

My pet mouse is called Ace.
He loves to eat out of my hand!

Take a glance at mice
once in a while!

Don't you think mice are nice?

CHECKING FOR MEANING

1. What are baby mice called? *(Literal)*
2. At what time of day do mice like to race about? *(Literal)*
3. Why do you think it is important that mice have space to play when they are kept as pets? *(Inferential)*
4. Do you agree with the author that mice are nice? Why? *(Evaluative)*

EXTENDING VOCABULARY

ice	What is ice made from? What does it feel like?
glance	Look at the word *glance*. How many sounds are in the word? What are those sounds? What word could the author have used instead of *glance* in the text?
nice	What is another word with a similar meaning to *nice*?

MOVING BEYOND THE TEXT

1. Would you like to own a pet mouse? Why?
2. What are some other animals whose babies are called pups? What other words for baby animals do you know?
3. How are mice similar to other common pets, such as cats or dogs? How are they different?
4. Why do you think some people are afraid of mice?

TIME TO WRITE

Imagine you are a mouse – a pet mouse or a wild mouse. Write a couple of sentences describing a day in your life.